Saber-Toothed Cats

by Susan E. Goodman

illustrations by
Kerry Maguire

For Dylan,
I hope you enjoy this
book about some AMAZING
cats. I hear *you love*
animals... me too!
They are my SCIENCE *"PAWS"ION!*

M Millbrook Press/Minneapolis

Enjoy! Kerry

I'd like to thank Larry D. Martin, senior curator of vertebrate paleontology at Kansas University Natural History Museum, for sharing his knowledge; and Christopher Shaw, collections manager at the Page Museum at the La Brea Tar Pits in Los Angeles, for his endless patience and expert review of my manuscript. Thanks to Kerry Maguire for bringing all these animals back to life, and to Shannon Barefield for shepherding this book through. —S.E.G.

Thanks to John M. Harris, chief curator of the Page Museum at the La Brea Tar Pits, and to Larry D. Martin of the Kansas University Natural History Museum, for their guidance. —K.M.

Text copyright © 2006 by Susan E. Goodman
Illustrations copyright © 2006 by Kerry Maguire

All rights reserved. International copyright secured. No part of this book may be reproduced, stored in a retrieval system, or transmitted in any form or by any means— electronic, mechanical, photocopying, recording, or otherwise—without the prior written permission of Lerner Publishing Group, except for the inclusion of brief quotations in an acknowledged review.

Millbrook Press
A division of Lerner Publishing Group
241 First Avenue North
Minneapolis, MN 55401 U.S.A.

Website address: www.lernerbooks.com

Library of Congress Cataloging-in-Publication Data

Goodman, Susan E., 1952–
    Saber-toothed cats / by Susan E. Goodman ; illustrations by Kerry Maguire.
      p.   cm. — (On my own science)
    ISBN-13: 978–1–57505–759–0 (lib. bdg. : alk. paper)
    ISBN-10: 1–57505–759–X (lib. bdg. : alk. paper)
    1. Saber-toothed tigers—Juvenile literature. I. Maguire, Kerry, ill. II. Title.
III. Series.
QE882.C15G66 2006
569'.74—dc22   2004013864

Manufactured in the United States of America
1 2 3 4 5 6 – DP – 11 10 09 08 07 06

*To Rayne and Shadow, who attack
their Seafood Supper as if it were
a mastodon or giant sloth*
—*S.E.G.*

*For loving husband, Rick, who gave
up our weekend dates so extra time
could be spent in the studio, and to
daughter Molly, my midnight elf*
—*K.M.*

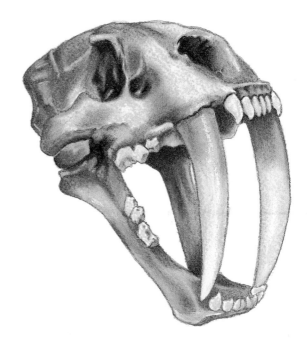

The Hunt
California, 13,000 years ago

The *Smilodon* were hungry.

It had been a long time since their last kill.

These saber-toothed cats

needed to hunt again.

The lead cat walked through the bushes.

The other cats followed.

They were looking, smelling, and

listening for their next meal.

CRACK! CRASH!

Smilodon were great hunters.

This time, it didn't take a great hunter

to know that another animal was near.

All the cats had to do was look.

A giant ground sloth held

a tree branch in its claws.

The sloth was eating leaves.

The sloth was a slow animal.

It would be easy to catch.

But its claws were long and sharp.

They could rip through an enemy.

The lead cat decided to look

for an easier meal.

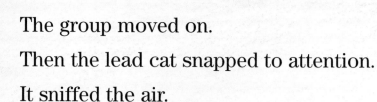

The group moved on.

Then the lead cat snapped to attention.

It sniffed the air.

Bison!

The cats sank down low.

Their spotted coats made them

hard to see in the grass.

The cats crept forward.

They watched and waited.

Finally, a young bison wandered
away from the herd.

The lead cat hid behind a rock.

The other cats fanned out
around their prey.

The bison was busy eating grass.

The cats crouched on their short back legs.

Their heavy shoulders twitched.

The lead cat burst out of hiding.

It ran right toward the bison.

The bison swerved away from the lead cat.

But it ran right toward the others!

One cat jumped onto its back.

The second cat sprang.

The cats dug their claws into
the bison and brought it down.

Then the lead cat caught up.

It opened its jaws wide.

Its sabers were like two long knives
ready to strike.

The cat stabbed its teeth
into the bison's belly.

The hunt was over.

Old Bones Can Talk

This story may show just how *Smilodon*
caught their bison dinner 13,000 years ago.
But it may not.
The truth is, scientists aren't sure how
Smilodon killed their prey.
They can only guess if these cats
hunted alone or in groups.

Scientists who study living animals learn by watching them and touching them.

Smilodon are not living animals.

They are extinct.

They died out about 11,000 years ago.

So scientists can never see how *Smilodon* lived.

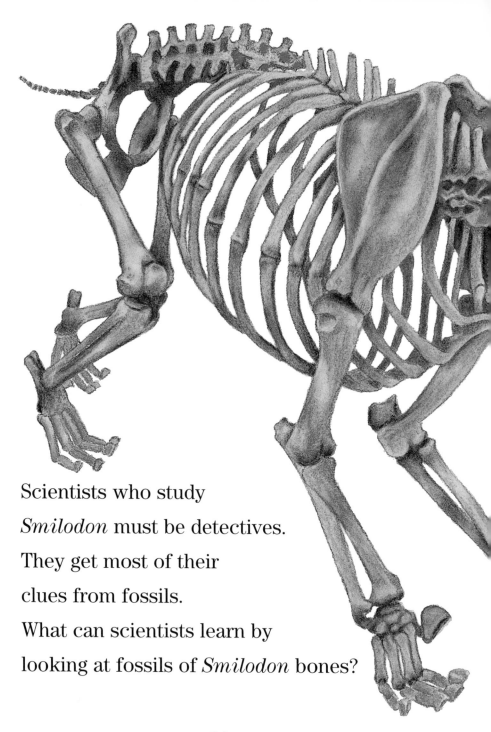

Scientists who study
Smilodon must be detectives.
They get most of their
clues from fossils.
What can scientists learn by
looking at fossils of *Smilodon* bones?

They can see that *Smilodon* had
short legs and a short tail.
Smilodon also had powerful
shoulders and front legs.
And it had a wicked pair
of sabers, 7 inches long.
Smilodon was smaller than a lion.
But its body was built more
like a bear's than a cat's.

Scientists use these clues to figure
out how *Smilodon* hunted.
They check their ideas by studying
how living animals look and move.
Cheetahs can run 70 miles an hour.
And they can run fairly far.
But cheetahs have light bodies.
They have long tails to help them balance.

Smilodon had a heavy body and a short tail.
Scientists think that *Smilodon* could
run about as fast as a brown bear.
That's 30 miles an hour.
But *Smilodon* couldn't run that
fast for very long.

Smilodon clearly couldn't chase
down prey like a cheetah does.
So how did *Smilodon* use its
heavy body to hunt?
All that weight could help *Smilodon*
knock down large animals.
Its strong shoulders could help it
wrestle animals to the ground.
Lions also use their weight
to pull down prey.
So some scientists think that
Smilodon hunted like lions do.
If that's true, *Smilodon* probably also
hunted in groups, just like lions.
They sneaked up on the animal,
jumped on it,
and knocked it over.

Then they used their sabers.
These teeth had tiny,
jagged edges
that could cut
like a saw.

Some scientists think that *Smilodon*
bit their victim's throat.
Others think that *Smilodon*
sliced the victim's belly.
Either way, the animal bled to death.

Then *Smilodon* settled in for a big meal.
Each cat could eat 50 pounds
of meat at one time.
That's like eating 150
hamburgers for dinner!

Did *Smilodon* live alone or in groups?
Scientists use fossils to try to
answer this question as well.
Some *Smilodon* fossils show that the
animals had terrible bite wounds
or broken legs.
Some of these fossils also show
that the cats lived long enough
to get better.

How could a cat that could
barely walk catch a bison?
How could a cat that couldn't hunt stay alive?
Some scientists think that these cats found
scraps of food left by other animals.
Other scientists believe that these fossils
prove that *Smilodon* lived in groups.
The groups' hunters may have brought
food to the injured cats.

Smilodon fossils tell us a lot.
But they cannot tell us everything.
What color was *Smilodon*'s
coat, for example?
In this case, scientists look to the
cat's home for answers.
Our *Smilodon* lived on plains
with grass, bushes, and trees.
Leaves made spotted shadows on the ground.

Some leopards live on plains like *Smilodon*'s.
Leopards have spotted coats that
blend in with shadows and plants.
Blending in helps leopards
sneak up on their prey.
Maybe *Smilodon* had a spotted coat
for the same reasons.
If you were a scientist, how would
you color *Smilodon*'s coat?

Smilodon's *World*

Smilodon lived in North America
and South America during the Ice Age.
This was a time when giant blankets of ice
covered the top part of the world.
The *Smilodon* in this story lived in
a place that wasn't covered with ice.
But it was very cold and rainy.
Smilodon shared its world with
other amazing animals.
It hunted many of them.
The giant ground sloth was one.
The sloth moved slowly.
But it had tiny, bony plates under its skin,
around its neck and back.
They made it hard for *Smilodon*
to bite into the sloth's throat.

Smilodon also hunted mammoths,
Ice Age relatives of elephants.
Healthy adult mammoths were too
big to kill, even for the fiercest cats.
Their tusks could grow 14 feet long.
That's as long as a car.
So *Smilodon* hunted young mammoths.

Mastodons looked a
lot like mammoths,
but they were smaller.
Still, the adult American
mastodon stood more than
10 feet high. It weighed
more than an elephant.

The long-horned bison was also huge.
A man could lie across its head,
touching one horn with his feet
and the other with his head.

Smilodon wasn't the only animal
that ate these plant eaters.
The dire wolf was a fierce hunter.
Its jaws and teeth were strong
enough to crush bones.

All of these animals are extinct.
No *Smilodon* or mammoths or
dire wolves still live on Earth.
Yet many animals from the
Ice Age are still alive.
Gray foxes still curl up in their dens.

Moles still feed
on earthworms.
Rattlesnakes still
soak up the sun.
Golden eagles still
soar in the sky.
Human beings survived
the Ice Age too.

Why did *Smilodon* and other
large animals die out?
Ice Age people started hunting
the big plant-eating animals too.
Some scientists think that humans
took too much of *Smilodon*'s food.
Most scientists blame the weather.
Our planet warmed up.
Warmer weather made different kinds
of plants and trees grow.
The big plant eaters didn't have
their normal foods.
They started to die out.
Smilodon couldn't catch the smaller,
faster animals that survived.
The time of the saber-toothed cat was over.

Beyond Smilodon

Smilodon wasn't the only
saber-toothed animal.
There were at least 35 other kinds
of cat-like animals with sabers.
These animals lived in many
parts of the world.
Some lived as long as 40 million years ago.
Barbourofelis fricki had the
longest sabers of any animal.
When it opened its jaws, its 9-inch
sabers were ready to strike.

Thylacosmilus had sabers that
kept growing and growing.
But these teeth never got longer
than about 5 inches.
That's because *Thylacosmilus*'s
lower teeth kept growing as well.
These bottom teeth rubbed
against the sabers to keep them
short and very, very sharp.

Three types of saber-toothed cats
lived in North America.
The bear-like *Smilodon* was one.
Homotherium was a different kind of cat.
It had long legs like a cheetah.
So *Homotherium* probably
chased down
its meals, like cheetahs do.

Homotherium's sabers were different from *Smilodon*'s. *Smilodon*'s sabers were long and thin with jagged edges. *Homotherium* had shorter sabers, but their edges were more jagged.

Xenosmilus also used to hunt
in North America.
Xenosmilus lived about
one million years ago.
It had a powerful body like *Smilodon*.
It had very jagged sabers like *Homotherium*.

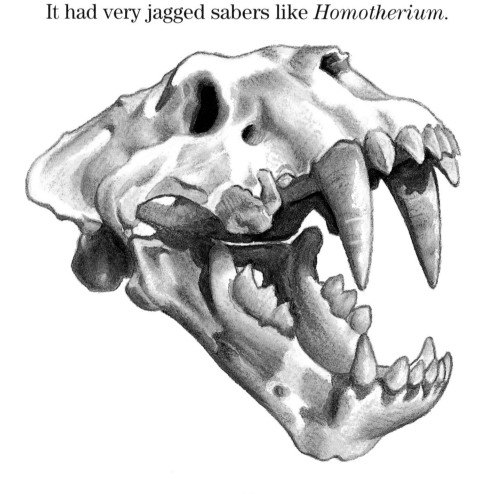

But *Xenosmilus* also had jagged
cutting edges on its other teeth.
When its sabers sliced into a victim,
its other teeth cut out
a huge chunk as well!

Fossil hunters have found the
bones of two *Xenosmilus*.
The bones were in the same place
as the fossils of many wild pigs.

Does this mean that the
two cats shared a den?
Did they hunt together and bring
their meat home with them?
If you were a scientist,
what would you do with these clues?

Glossary

extinct (eks-TINKT): when an animal or plant has died out forever

fossils (FAH-suhlz): the remains or traces of a plant or animal from long ago that have been preserved in the earth or in rock

Ice Age: a time when ice covered a lot of Earth's surface. Earth's past includes several Ice Ages.

prehistoric (pree-hihs-TOHR-ihk): something that happened in the time before written history

prey (PRAY): an animal that is hunted by another animal for food

sabers (SAY-buhrz): long, sharp teeth that are shaped like a type of curved sword called a saber

Learn More about Prehistoric Times

Goodman, Susan E. *On This Spot: An Expedition Back through Time.* New York: Greenwillow Books, 2004.

Hehner, Barbara. *Ice Age Cave Bear: The Giant Beast That Terrified Humans.* New York: Crown Books for Young Readers, 2002.

Kerley, Barbara. *The Dinosaurs of Waterhouse Hawkins.* New York: Scholastic, Inc., 2001.

Lessem, Don. *Giant Meat-Eating Dinosaurs.* Minneapolis: Lerner Publications Company, 2005.

Levy, Elizabeth. *Who Are You Calling a Woolly Mammoth?: Prehistoric America.* New York: Scholastic, Inc., 2001.

Walker, Sally M. *Mystery Fish: Secrets of the Coelacanth.* Minneapolis: Millbrook Press, 2006.

Walker, Sally M. *SuperCroc Found.* Minneapolis: Millbrook Press, 2006.

Selected Bibliography

Agusti, Jordí. *Mammoths, Sabertooths, and Hominids.* New York: Columbia University Press, 2002.

Alderton, David. *Wild Cats of the World.* New York: Facts on File, Inc., 2002.

Barton, Miles. *Prehistoric America: A Journey through the Ice Age and Beyond.* New Haven, CT: Yale University Press, 2002.

Turner, Alan. *The Big Cats and Their Fossil Relatives: An Illustrated Guide to Their Evolution and Natural History.* New York: Columbia University Press, 1997.